by
Émilie BEAUMONT

Illustrated by
Lindsey SELLEY

· DISCOVERING ANIMALS ·

SEA CREATURES

by
Émilie Beaumont

Illustrated by
Lindsey Selley

TRODDY
BOOKS

Whales

Although they live in the sea, whales are mammals. Most mammals are animals that live on land. They breathe air, and their babies feed on their mother's milk. Whales have to swim up to the surface to breathe. They breathe in and out through blowholes on top of their heads. Baby whales, called calves, feed on their mother's milk just like the babies of land mammals. Whales make many different sounds, which travel a long way through the water. We do not know what these sounds mean, but other whales understand them.

Whale's blowhole

The blue whale

There are two kinds of whales, toothed whales and baleen whales. Baleen whales, such as the blue whale, have no teeth. Instead, they have screens or filters in their mouths, which catch millions of tiny shrimps, called krill, for the whale's dinner. As the whale swims, sucking in water and blowing it out again, it swallows millions of these tiny creatures. In summer, the blue whale swims in the cold seas near the Arctic and Antarctic. In winter it moves to warmer seas. It lives alone, or with its calf.

The blue whale is the largest animal on Earth. It weighs more than 20 elephants.

Killer whale

The killer whale, or orca, is small for a whale. It weighs only about one tonne! In the ocean, it is a fierce hunter, and chases seals or large fish. It will even upset small boats. But this fierce animal can be tamed. Like all whales, it has a large brain, and it seems to like human beings. It enjoys doing tricks in zoos or aquariums.

Whalebone

The filters that some whales have instead of teeth are made of baleen, or whalebone. It is very tough but can bend, like the bristles of a brush, and it acts as a strainer. The whale takes in a big mouthful of water, then blows it out again. Millions of tiny animals and plants, called plankton, are caught inside its mouth.

Whales have warm blood, like all mammals. Land mammals have fur to keep them warm, but whales have thick layers of fat.

The sperm whale

This is a toothed whale. It has lots of large teeth, but only on its lower jaw. It is easy to recognise by its huge head, which takes up one-third of its body. A big sperm whale weighs about ten tonnes. It can stay under water for about 45 minutes before it needs to breathe, and it can dive a mile deep. Its main food is squid or octopus.

Dolphins

Dolphins belong to the whale family. They are mammals too, although they are smaller than most whales. A dolphin grows to two or three metres long.

They are very strong swimmers. At full speed, they can reach 70 kph, and they travel long distances at about 30 kph.

You often see them swimming along with ships. They seem to like people. Sometimes a dolphin will stay near a beach and play with people swimming.

Baby dolphins

Young dolphins are called calves. They are usually born in the spring, and the mother dolphin has only one baby at a time.

A dolphin's skin is very smooth. If you stroke it, it feels like silk.

A young dolphin likes to play with its mother.

Dolphins will sometimes jump out of the water and dive through the waves. They almost seem to be dancing.

It stays close to her, and feeds on her milk. She keeps a watch for sharks, which often attack young dolphins.

Some dolphins live in fresh water. They live in large rivers, like the Ganges in India and the Amazon in South America. These fresh-water dolphins have long beaks full of strong teeth for crunching shellfish (see the picture below). They can hardly see, but find their food by listening and by smell.

Dolphins are sometimes called porpoises. The seas contain many different kinds.

Talking dolphins

Dolphins 'talk' to one another by means of little cries and whistles. They also make sounds so high that a human ear cannot hear them. By sending out sounds and listening for echoes, dolphins track down fish to eat. They find their way through the ocean in the same way.

The friendly dolphin

Because dolphins are very intelligent, they can be trained easily. They seem to enjoy showing off. With the help of their powerful tails, they can 'stand' on the water for a few seconds, and even move backwards.

9

The Octopus

In old stories about the sea, the octopus, or squid, was a terrible monster. It dragged sailors down to the bottom of the sea, and squeezed divers to death with its long arms, or tentacles. These stories are unfair! Although giant squid do exist in very deep waters, they hardly ever attack divers. They are shy animals. Anything strange, like a human diver, makes them swim for a safe hiding place. With its soft body, the octopus can hide in cracks in the rocks. It can even change its colour, so its enemies will not notice it.

A bolt hole

The octopus make its home in a hole, protected by rocks and weeds. Any safe place will do, even inside a sunken ship or an old barrel.

A fight with an eel

An octopus may try to make its home in the same hole as a Moray eel. The eel may be smaller, but it has strong, sharp teeth. It usually wins the fight with the octopus. Sometimes two octopuses fight to decide which one is the owner of the hole.

Tentacles

The octopus has eight arms, or tentacles. Each one is covered with suckers. It can grasp crabs, which are its main food, very firmly. It crunches them up in its powerful jaws.

The eggs of the octopus

An octopus lays eggs. It may do this only once in its life, but it lays thousands of eggs at that time. They hang in bunches, like grapes, and the octopus keeps guard over them until they hatch.She guards them so well that she sometimes forgets to feed herself.

A cloud of ink

When an octopus is in danger, it lets out a cloud of black, inky liquid. The ink cloud hides it from its enemy, and gives it time to escape.

The octopus crawls along the bottom of the sea, but it can also swim. It uses a kind of jet to push itself along. It has many enemies, including fishermen who catch it in nets or traps. Sharks, dolphins, sperm whales, eels and other big fish will also eat it if they can.

Fish

Thousands of different kinds of fish live in the sea. They swim with the muscles in their sides, bending their bodies from side to side. The tail helps them to swim and to steer. Other fins help them keep their balance. The skin of most fish is covered with hard scales, and the scales are protected by a coating of sticky liquid. As it swims, a fish takes in water through its mouth and lets it out through its gills, which are slits in the side of its head. The gills take oxygen from the water, just as our lungs take oxygen from the air we breathe.

A ray

The ray is a flatfish

It has both eyes in the top of its head and fins on the sides of its body. When it is not swimming, it lies on the bottom of the sea. It is very hard to see, as it covers itself with sand. If you are paddling in the sea and you feel the bottom move, you may have stepped on a ray!

Whale shark

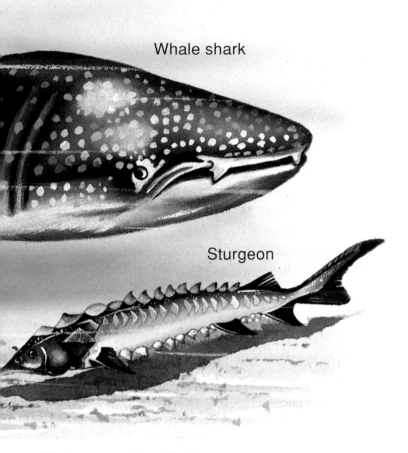

Sturgeon

Flying fish

The little flying fish has a good way of escaping from its enemies. It swims up to the surface at great speed, and its wide fins carry it through the air for several metres.

Fish come in all sizes. The smallest are less than one centimetre long. The biggest is the whale shark, which can grow up to 20 m long. Although it is a shark, it is not a fierce creature, and eats only plankton.

Most fish live for five years or more. Some reach 20 years. The fish that lives longest is the sturgeon, which lives partly in the sea and partly in rivers. It can live for nearly 100 years.

Baby fish that have just been hatched are called fry.

Parrot fish

Parrot fish have very hard jaws. They can even bite through coral, which is as hard as rock. They live among coral reefs, and when they are resting they make a kind of thin blanket to cover themselves, like a layer of clingfilm.

All fish lay eggs. Some lay their eggs on the sandy bottom. Others fix them to seaweed, or let them float in the water.

Salmon

Any fishermen will tell you that the salmon is the king of fish. It is strong and handsome, and it leads an amazing life. Like sturgeon, salmon spend part of their lives in rivers and part in the sea. As young fish, they leave the rivers where they were born and swim thousands of miles through the ocean. Several years later, they return to lay their eggs. They always return to the river where they were born. Salmon, which grow up to two metres long, need clean water to lay their eggs. Today, many rivers are so dirty that the salmon cannot use them.

When salmon leave the sea to go up the river, some changes happen. They turn a reddish colour, and the male fish grows a hook on its jaw.

A brave fish

The salmon finds its own river by smell. To a salmon, every river that flows into the sea has its own smell. When it finds the river, it must swim up it to lay its eggs in the shallow water far upstream. This is not an easy journey. Many dangers and difficulties lie in wait. But salmon are very strong swimmers. They

When the salmon have laid their eggs, they return to the sea. Because they are so tired by their efforts, some die. Others reach the sea, where they soon grow strong again.

can swim against fast currents and even jump up a waterfall. If a dam has been built across the river, a fish 'ladder' is built too. It has pools along it, so the salmon can rest during its hard, uphill swim.

The female lays her eggs

The eggs are laid on the gravel bottom, where the river is shallow. She can lay 2000 eggs, but many are eaten by birds or fish. When the baby salmon are hatched, they spend two years in the river before setting out to sea.

Salmon farms

Salmon are very good to eat, and today they are raised in salmon farms. The young salmon are kept in pens near the sea. Nets prevent them swimming away. They are given plenty of food, so they grow fast.

Sharks

People are frightened of sharks, because big sharks can attack and kill human beings. But most sharks are not dangerous. Out of about 250 different kinds of shark, only about 20 are dangerous to people. The largest of all sharks, the whale shark, is a peaceful fish that eats nothing bigger than a shrimp or a small fish. The great white shark is much smaller but not so peaceful. People have been attacked by white sharks (but far more white sharks have been killed by people).

Sharks have nothing to do except swim and eat. They eat at any time, day or night. Squid or octopus is one of their favourite foods, but they also eat fish, seals, and even other sharks. They are not very intelligent and they are not frightened of anything, so they will eat all kinds of strange things. Lumps of wood

The blue shark is one of the most beautiful fish in the sea, with a dark blue skin and smooth shape. It is a hunting shark and grows up to seven metres long, so it can be dangerous. It has seven rows of sharp teeth in its jaws.

Sharks don't need dentists

Its teeth are the only weapon of a hunting shark. It has several rows of them, and they are often broken or lost. When teeth are lost, new ones quickly take their place.

Dolphin attack

Sharks eat young dolphins, if they can catch them. Sometimes, a group of dolphins will attack a shark. They swim towards it at full speed and ram it with their hard noses.

and bits of old motor cars are some of the things that have been found inside a shark's stomach. The mouth of a shark is underneath its head, so it must turn on its side to bite. Some sharks have jaws which push forward when they bite, so they can swallow a fish almost as big as themselves.

Sawshark

Hammerhead

Strange heads

The sawshark has a very long snout with teeth along the edges. It uses it to slash at the fish it eats. Another shark with a very strange head is the hammerhead. Its head is shaped like the letter T, and its eyes are at the ends of the crossbar of the T.

Fish we eat

On these pages are pictures of some of the fish that are caught for human beings to eat. There are about 20,000 kinds of fish that are good to eat. These are a few of the most common ones. Every year, fishing boats catch about 60 million fish. The supply never runs out, because the seas are so rich. All the same, some kinds of fish are not so common as they were years ago. Too many have been caught. The herring is one example. A herring from the North Sea once cost a penny. Now, herring fishing has almost stopped.

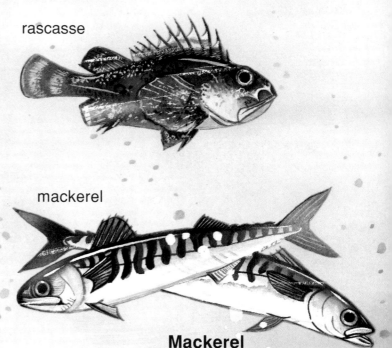

rascasse

mackerel

Mackerel

Mackerel are easy to recognize because they have stripes, like a zebra. They swim in large shoals. When a fisherman catches one, he knows he will catch more in the same place.

Cod

Cod swim in large groups, called shoals, in the cold waters of the North Atlantic. In England, cod is often the fish you buy in fish-and-chip shops.

cod

sole

Turbot and sole

These are both flatfish, with eyes in the top of their heads. They swim by moving their bodies up and down in rippling movements. When resting, they take shelter in the sand on the bottom of the sea.

turbot

Rascasse

This is not a pretty fish, but it is tasty. In countries on the Mediterranean Sea, it is made into fish stew.

Sardine

We know these little fish best in tins. They swim in big shoals, and fishermen catch thousands at one time.

sardine

mullet

whiting

Mullet

There are many kinds of mullet, such as grey mullet and red mullet. In parts of Africa, fishermen catch them with the help of dolphins. They beat the water with sticks. Dolphins swim towards the sound, and drive the mullet into the fishermen's nets.

Whiting

Whiting are common fish in cold seas. They taste like cod, but they are smaller.

Tuna

Most tuna grow to about one metre long. The red tuna, which is caught in the Mediterranean and the Atlantic, is bigger. It can grow to three metres and weighs nearly one tonne. Tuna are fast, strong swimmers. They travel for very long distances in the oceans.

tuna

Odd Fish

The sea contains some very strange fish. Some of them live in the deepest parts, in complete darkness. There are probably some fish and other creatures living in the deepest parts of the ocean which no one has seen yet. Some funny-looking fish are shown on these pages. Don't let them give you bad dreams!

Flying rascasse

This is a really pretty fish, with its red stripes. But watch out for those spines. They are poisonous.

Cow fish

This fat little fish has tiny horns sticking out from its head.

Frog fish

There are many kinds of frog fish. They live among thick seaweed.

This frog fish has fins under its stomach which it rests on, as if they were feet.

This one really does look like a fat frog. It is hard to see when it hides among the rocks.

Porcupine fish

When it is frightened, the porcupine fish blows itself up with water. That makes its spines stick out. Porcupine fish live in all the warmer seas.

Balloon fish

This is another fish that can blow itself up so that it looks larger than it really is.

Viper fish

Fish that live deep in the ocean often have large, sharp teeth. The viper fish is one. It has spots on its body that glow. When small fish come near, the viper fish snaps them up.

Scorpion fish

21

Crustaceans

Crabs, lobsters and shrimps all belong to the family of animals called Crustaceans. They have shells, which do not grow as the animal inside them grows. When a crustacean grows too big for its shell, it sheds it, as a snake sheds its skin. Then it grows a new, larger one. Some crustaceans change their shells eight times before they are five years old. When it sheds its shell, the crustacean has no defence against fish that want to eat it. So it hides itself in a hole and waits for the new shell to grow hard.

The largest lobster ever caught was one metre long and weighed 20 kg.

fiddler crab

Lobsters

Lobsters have large claws, or pincers, which they use to catch their food. One claw is bigger than the other. Lobsters can be bad-tempered. They sometimes fight each other, and they may attack fish like eels when they meet them in cracks in the rocks.

crayfish

lobster

hermit crab

Crustaceans lay eggs, like fish. When the eggs hatch, the larvae that come out look nothing like their parents. They change their form several times while they are growing up.

The shrimp and its eggs

The female shrimp carries her eggs under her body for several months.

The crayfish looks like a lobster, but it has no big claws. The long feelers on its head help it find its way around.

The spider crab has a small body and long legs.

Crabs all have pincers, like the lobster. If you pick up a crab, hold it just behind its pincers. If you don't, it may give you a nip.

The hermit crab has no shell of its own. It looks for an empty shell, and lives in that.

spider crab

edible crab

Sharing a home

The tiny pea crab lives inside the shell of a mussel. It is safe there, and the mussel does not mind because the pea crab cleans up old scraps of food. It is a good housekeeper.

Some crabs hide from their enemies by digging into the sand. Others hide in cracks in the rocks and cover themselves with seaweed.

Shellfish

Mussels

Mussels live on rocks. They fix themselves to the rock with small threads, so the tide cannot wash them off.

mussels

Scallops

Scallops spend most of their time lying on the sand. When an enemy, like a starfish, comes near, they move away at a surprising speed. They swim by taking water into their shells, then driving it out through small gaps at the back.

scallops

Cockles and clams

These shellfish hide from their enemies by digging into the sand. Like scallops, they swim by passing water through their shells.

cockles

Razorfish

The shell of the razorfish looks like an old-fashioned razor. Razorfish have one powerful foot. They use it to dig a hole in the sand.

razorfish

24

Limpets

Limpets fix themselves to rocks with suckers. They are fixed very firmly, and it is hard to pull one off. When the tide comes in and covers them, it brings tiny scraps of seaweed, which the limpets eat.

Oysters

In some oysters you may find pearls. When a grain of sand gets into its shell, the oyster covers it with a smooth, pearly substance to stop it scratching. It adds more layers, and so a pearl is made.

oysters

Winkles and whelks

These shellfish are sea snails. They can hide inside their shells, and close a little door.

Screwshells

Screwshells are just the right shape to screw themselves into the sand.

limpets

screwshells

winkles

clams

whelks

Turtles

All turtles are sea animals. Their relations which live on land are called tortoises. Some turtles are very large, weighing more than 500 kg. They live in warm seas, but lay their eggs on land. Once, they were hunted for their meat and shells, but no hunting is allowed today. The turtles are carefully protected. On the beaches where they go to lay eggs, guards watch over them. The guards make sure the turtles get back to the sea safely.

Turtles always lay their eggs on the same beach. Sometimes they swim for thousands of kilometres to get to the right beach. The female turtle lays the eggs, so male turtles never have to leave the water.

The turtle's eggs

The turtle lays her eggs in a deep hole, which she digs in the sand with her flippers. When the eggs are laid, she covers them with sand to hide them. The eggs hatch about two months later. The babies have a special spike, like a tooth, which grows on their heads. With this, they break through the shell. Then they push through the sand to reach the air.

Return to the sea

Turtles are strong swimmers in the sea, but on land they move with great difficulty because they are so heavy. When the female turtle has laid her eggs in the sand high on the beach, she turns back to the sea at once. But she is very tired after laying all those eggs. She needs all her strength to reach the safety of the water. When the baby turtles are hatched, they also hurry to the sea. They are not so heavy, but their journey is still dangerous. Crabs, birds and giant lizards wait for them, hoping to find an easy meal.

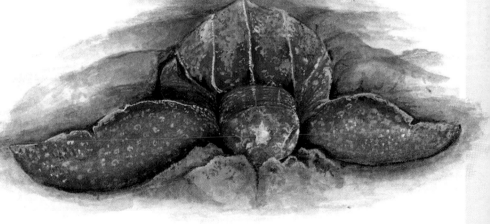

Turtles live for a long time, 100 years or more.

Trapped by mud

If the beach is very wet or muddy, the tired mother turtle cannot drag herself down to the sea. She becomes stuck in the muddy sand. She will soon die if no one helps her. Luckily, the guards who keep watch will help her get back to the sea.

CONTENTS

Typeset by TPS Ltd, London

This edition published in 1992 by
Regency House Publishing Limited
The Grange
Grange Yard
London
SE1 3AG

Printed in Italy
ISBN 1 85361 306 1